*Watch for these additional Holiday Books
written by the same author:*
**THE PUMPKIN BOOK
THE THANKSGIVING BOOK
THE ELVES CHRISTMAS BOOK**

PUMPKIN PRESS

PUBLISHING HOUSE

P.O. Box 139
Shasta, CA 96087

The Bunny Book

FULL OF SPRINGTIME HISTORY, POEMS, SONGS, ART PROJECTS, GAMES AND RECIPES

For Parents and Teachers to use
with young Children.

Written and Illustrated by
SUSAN OLSON HIGGINS

PUMPKIN PRESS

PUBLISHING HOUSE

P.O. Box 139
Shasta, CA 96087

Written and Published by Susan Olson Higgins
  Pumpkin Press, P.O. Box 139, Shasta, CA 96087

Dedicated to all of the eggs I never found...

and to Margaret and Peter Olson,
my grandmother and grandfather,
who filled me with their love.

I would like to extend baskets FULL of thank-you's to Dan Higgins, Jane Williams, Linda Jones, Florence Higgins, Dick Burns, Mary Burns, Joyce Huber, and Ruth Begalke for their contributions and suggestions included in **THE BUNNY BOOK.**

I would especially like to thank V.I. Wexner for editing this edition.

PREFACE

As Spring bursts into bloom, it brings new life to the earth and one of the most blessed holidays of the year... Easter!

Within these pages are history, poems, songs, art projects, games, and recipes for you to use as you try to capture the Spring-sproingy, bunny-fun of this season.

Have a happy-hoppy Easter!

Susan Olson Higgins

SH-H-H-H! This EASTER HINT is a secret!

At home on Easter morning while the children are sleeping, or in your classroom while the children are outside, mark the Easter Bunny's path so the children can follow his muddy footprints when they come into the room. It is very simple. Here is how you do it:

*Put two or three tablespoons of dirt into a small container.

*Mix a few drops of water until it is muddy.

*Using two fingers, mark a path of bunny tracks around the room — starting where the bunny would enter, of course.

*Be sure to leave the eggs or set a basket in clear view for the children to find as a token of the bunny's visit.

TABLE OF CONTENTS

THE HISTORY OF EASTER

Easter is a religious holiday celebrated each year by Christians to commemorate the resurrection of Jesus Christ. It honors Christ's victory over death when, on the third day after His crucifixion on the cross, He rose from the dead and took away the sins of the world. An angel appeared to His followers and announced, "He is risen."

Easter is celebrated on varying Sundays between March 22 and April 25. It is called a movable feast. It was Roman emperor Constantine who ruled in 325 A.D. that Easter should be celebrated on the first Sunday after the full moon following the spring equinox. Should the full moon occur on a Sunday which coincides with Passover, a festival celebrated by the Jews, then Easter should be commemorated on the following Sunday. This settled any disputes about celebrating the two feasts on the same day. However, there remained a discrepancy over which calendar to use when deciding the dates. So, even today, Easter is celebrated on different days in different parts of the world.

How the name Easter came about is lost in history. Some researchers believe that its name came from an Anglo-Saxon goddess of spring named Easter, or the festival in her honor called Eostur. That was a festival celebrating the coming of Spring at the time of the vernal equinox. That, of course, is the same time of year Easter is celebrated.

EASTER TRADITIONS AND SYMBOLS

EGGS

Of course, eggs represent new life. Long ago, some people believed that the earth was hatched from a gigantic egg! Eggs have been exchanged for centuries. Ancient Egyptians dyed eggs and gave them to friends as gifts. In England, friends wrote messages on colored eggs. The practice of coloring and exchanging eggs has been carried on in many parts of the world today. Some of the most elaborately decorated eggs are Ukranian, from Eastern Europe. Often eggs are left by the Easter bunny for children to find on Easter morning, much to their delight!

EASTER RABBITS

In America and around the world, many children believe that the Easter bunny brings Easter eggs and hides them for finding on Easter morning. Where did this tradition begin? There are many different legends, but here is a popular one:

Long ago in Germany there lived an old, loving woman who adored children. Each year she would give the children gifts to celebrate spring. One year she had nothing to give because she had grown very poor due to a great famine in the land. All she had were some eggs. She did not want to disappoint the children, so quickly before they arrived for their gifts, she colored the eggs and hid them in the grass. When the children came, she told them to run out into the lawn to find their gifts hiding there. Of course, the children ran into the yard in search of their surprise. Just as one of the children uncovered the eggs, a large rabbit hopped away. So the children thought that the rabbit had left the eggs for them! And ever since, children have searched for the eggs left by the Easter rabbit on Easter morning.

Here's another truth: In ancient Egypt, the rabbit symbolized the moon. It also represented new life and birth. Because Easter's date is determined by the moon, and Easter occurs in the spring-time, it was natural that the rabbit continued to be one of the symbols of Easter.

EASTER THROUGHOUT THE WORLD

SPAIN

In Spain, cities hold religious processions through the streets. Priests wear special garb and men carry large, life-size wooden images which represent Christ's life and the last few days before the crucifiction.

GERMANY

In Germany, it is traditional to eat cake and pretzels at Easter time. People carry colored eggs all through the day for good luck. This is the country where the tradition of hiding eggs began. There are also egg rolling contests — the winner can win over one hundred eggs.

ENGLAND

They have a custom where the children join hands and cirlce around the church with their backs to it. Then the children "clip" or embrace the church.

GREECE

In Greece, the people dress in their national costume and enjoy music and dancing on Easter Monday. On Good Friday before Easter, four men from the community carry a wooden cross and figure of Christ in a procession through the streets, with the congregation following. Later, they return to the church where they receive flowers and candles blessed by the priest.

UKRAINE

In the Ukraine, people celebrate Easter for two weeks. This is where the famously decorated eggs originate. Each village creates its own design. Often, decorated egg shells are cast on the water to show the dead that it is Easter.

MEXICO

In Mexico, thousands of people fill the streets on the afternoon before Easter. They hit and burn images of Judas Iscariot, the man who betrayed Jesus. Often, Judas' image was a pinata filled with candy. When it is broken open with a stick, candy falls to the ground, much to the delight of the children.

MIDDLE EAST

Often church officials invite beggars off the street into their churches to wash their feet and offer them gifts in memory of Christ.

PASSOVER

Passover is an ancient Jewish holiday which comes in the spring and celebrates the Israelites' escape from Egyptian slavery. In the Old Testament, it is explained that an angel of the Lord instructed the Israelites to mark their homes with lambs' blood so their first born would be passed over and spared. Nowadays, at family feasts, called *seders*, children recall the lessons of history, and eat special foods, like *matzohs*, a flat bread similar to the crackers eaten in the desert more than three thousand years ago.

WHEN SPRING HAS SPRUNG

The vernal equinox is the first day of the season spring. It falls on March 21. That is when the sun is directly over the equator. On this date, day and night are equal length over the entire earth. It is a time of year that the greatest changes occur on a day to day basis in the length of day and night. The word vernal is a derivative of the Latin term "greening", which, of course, occurs in spring. Equi means equal. Nox means night. All together, they do imply equal day and night at this spring time of year.

BUNNY POEMS

OFF TO BED NOW!
by Susan Olson Higgins

Did You Know...
The Easter bunny never arrives
Until you're in bed and you close your eyes.

He never visits a child who's awake.
So go right to sleep...for your own sake.

If you go right to sleep, he will hide some treats.
He will fill your basket with eggs and sweets.

He always knows if you've gone to bed,
So hop right in and cover your head;

While you are sleeping, that's when bunny brings
All those delicious Eastery things.

YOU CAN BE A BUNNY
by Susan Olson Higgins

Sniff, sniff, sniff,
            (sniff three times)
Hop, hop, hop,
            (hop three times)
Shake your little bunny tail,
            (shake your backside)
Then stop, stop, stop.
            (stand quietly)

Twitch, twitch, twitch,
            (twitch nose three times)
Hop out of sight,
            (hop to another part of room)
Crawl into your bunny burrow for the night
            (snuggle into "burrow" and sleep)

A BUNNY TAIL
by Susan Olson Higgins

It is little
And fluffy,
White
And puffy.

It is short
And shaggy,
And not
Very waggy.

It sits
On the end
And can hardly
Bend.

It is soft
And round
And all you can see as away bunny bounds.

11

A BUNNY WHO IS FUNNY
by Susan Olson Higgins

I know an Easter bunny who is oh so funny...

He stands six feet tall,
His whiskers curl around,
His ears stand high
At the slightest sound.

He wears a green vest
And a pink bow tie.
If he flaps his ears...
You should see him fly!

He can bend and twist
Into any shape at all.
He can hop or skip
Or curl up like a ball.

He has a gold watch
Which he keeps very near,
But he only has use for it
In Spring each year.

And as for eggs...
Well, he has a lot.
All children want
What he has got!

He is very, very clever,
And as quick as can be.
I hope he never, NEVER
Stops visiting me!

LITTLE CHICKS
by Susan Olson Higgins

Little chicks
Yellow fluff,
Flap their wings
Ruffle ruff.

They peck their corn,
Delicious stuff,
Then march about
Puff, puff, puff.

(This can be used as action poem.)

A SPRING-SPROINGY DAY
by Susan Olson Higgins

It's Spring, Spring, Sproing, Spring!
Birds are back to chirp and sing.

It's Spring, Spring! Flowers are up.
The tulips and violets and butterycups.

It's Spring. It's Spring! Run out to play
Under the sun on this Spring-sproingy day.

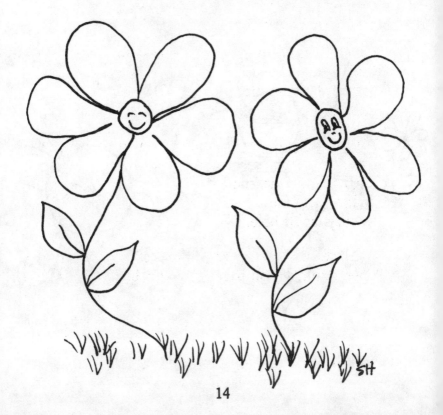

14

A BUNNY FINGER PLAY
by Susan Olson Higgins

Five little bunnies   *(hold up five fingers)*
Hopped up a hill.
One stopped to gather
A yellow jonquil.

Four little bunnies   *(hold up four fingers)*
Hopped past me.
One stopped to nibble
By the old willow tree.

Three little bunnies   *(hold up three fingers)*
Hopped near a brook.
One heard a splash
And stopped to take a look.

Two little bunnies   *(hold up two fingers)*
Hopped past a mouse.
One stopped to visit
In his teeny-tiny house.

One little bunny   *(hold up one finger then
     have it "hop" behind your back)*
Hopped down the knoll.
He disappeared in
His cozy rabbit hole.

You might wish to try the art project, "Five Finger
Puppet Bunnies" on page 38 of this book.

SIGNS OF SPRING
by Susan Olson Higgins

A lady bug,
A tiny bud,
Snow that's melting
Into mud.

A woolly lamb,
Some purple hills,
A garden full
Of daffodils.

A frisky colt,
A bumble bee,
Fresh pink blossoms
On a tree.

A pussy willow,
A chick's peep, peep,
A fat green frog
Awakes from sleep.

A butterfly
Flits here and there,
Signs of Spring
Are everywhere.

And as far
As can be seen,
Fields and valleys
New mown green.

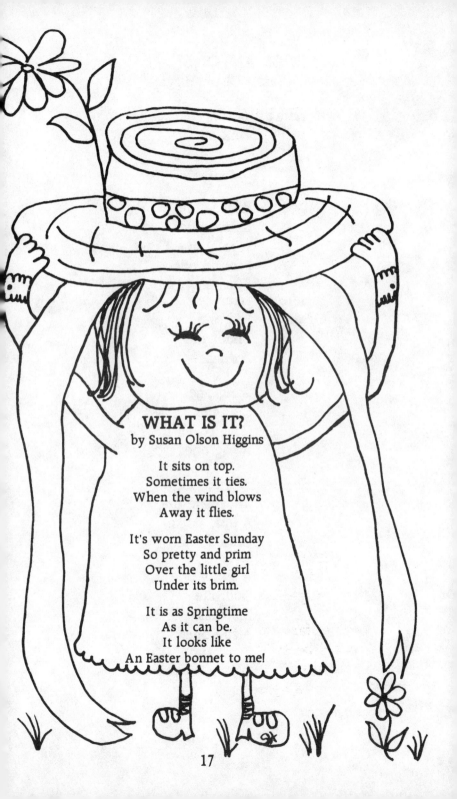

WHAT IS IT?
by Susan Olson Higgins

It sits on top.
Sometimes it ties.
When the wind blows
Away it flies.

It's worn Easter Sunday
So pretty and prim
Over the little girl
Under its brim.

It is as Springtime
As it can be.
It looks like
An Easter bonnet to me!

17

EGGS ANYONE?
by Susan Olson Higgins

Here's a fat one
  Pink one
  Orange one
  Clown one.

  A little one
  Round one
  A rolly one
  I found one!

Here's a green one
  Red one
  Under the
  Bed one.

  A zig one
  Zag one
  Covered with
  A bag one.

Here's a spotted one
  Chocolate one
  A blue polka-
  Dotted one.

  A shiny one
  Dull one
  My basket is
  A full one.

I FOUND HIM!
by Susan Olson Higgins

Way out back where the butterflies pass,
Lies a sleeping bunny in the soft green grass.

He is snuggled under tulips and daffodil leaves.
His fur waves and ruffles in the gentle breeze.

He is lying there so quietly in that sunny spot.
He makes me wonder if he is . . . or not.

I don't see his basket or any eggs around,
Or any purple jelly beans hiding on the ground.

But, I'm sure. Very sure. Just as sure as can be.
This is the Easter bunny right in front of me!

EASTER RIDDLES
by Susan Olson Higgins

I hop and I jump
My ears are big and funny.
My tail is puffy,
I am the Easter . . . *(bunny)*.

I waddle and quack
And with any luck
I will catch a fat bug.
I'm an Easter . . . *(duck)*.

I am oval in shape.
I can roll through your legs.
I am colored, then hidden,
I am an Easter . . . *(egg)*.

Where corn is about
I pick, peck, pick.
I come from an egg.
I am an Easter . . . *(chick)*.

HOPPY BUNNY
(action poem)
by Susan Olson Higgins

Hop, hop, hop to the left. *(hop left)*
Hop, hop to the right. *(hop right)*
Easter Bunny hide your eggs, *(pretend to hide eggs)*
Then hop, hop out of sight. *(quietly hop away)*

THE EASTER EGG HUNT (action poem)
by Susan Olson Higgins

Look around
Reach out
Bend over
Give a shout. (Here's one!)

Stretch high
Bend low
Reach under
Stand up slow.

Pick it up
Put it in
Hold your basket
Turn and spin.

Stoop over
Straighten legs
Find a spot to
Count your eggs!

1, 2, 3, 4, 5, 6, 7, 8, 9, 10!

SPRING RIDDLE
by Susan Olson Higgins

All through the winter they quietly sleep.
When Spring arrives, up they creep.
Slowly, so slowly, they poke up their heads.
They dress in bright colors, but stay in their beds.

They bend and bow and nod to the breeze
And gather all of the sunshine they please.
They drink up the water that falls from the sky,
Then chat contentedly as bees buzz by.
Who are they? *(flowers)*

HERE SITS A BUNNY (finger play)
by Susan Olson Higgins

Here sits a bunny.
> *(Make a fist. Hold up two fingers for bunny ears)*

Here sits a chick.
> *(Make a fist with other hand. Extend thumb and pointer for beak)*

Bunny ears wiggle.
> *(Wiggle bunny ears)*

Chick's beak clicks.
> *(Open and close chick's beak)*

Hop away bunny.
> *(Bounce bunny hand to knee)*

Run away chick.
> *(Chick runs to other knee)*

Bunny nibble nibbles.
> *(Wiggle ears as bunny nibbles)*

Chick pick picks.
> *(Chick's beak pecks knee)*

QUESTIONS   by Susan Olson Higgins

Where does the chick, chick, come from, come from?
Where does the little chick come from?
> Does he come from the elf?
> Or from grandpa's shelf?
> Does he come from the store?
> Or the ocean shore?

Where does the chick, chick, come from, come from?
Where does the little chick come from?

Where does the little egg come from, come from?
Where does the little egg come from?
> Does it come from the moon?
> Or the giant's spoon?
> Does it come from the brook?
> Come and help me look!

Where does the little egg come from, come from?
Where does the little egg come from?

SILLY LITTLE BUNNY
(action poem)
by Susan Olson Higgins

Silly little bunny
Wrinkle your nose. *(wrinkle nose)*
Bend down low *(bend down)*
And touch your toes. *(touch toes)*

> Now little bunny
> Stand up tall. *(stand)*
> Wiggle your ears. *(wiggle hands over head)*
> Don't let them fall!

Happy little bunny
Spin around. *(spin around)*
Show where your cotton tail
Can be found. *(wiggle backside)*

> Hurry little bunny
> Jump up high. *(jump up)*
> Hop away before
> Easter passes by! *(hop away)*

BUNNY SONGS

TO TUNES YOU KNOW

SPRINGTIME FLOWERS

by Susan Olson Higgins
(tune: Ring-A-Ring-A-Roses)

A ring of springtime flowers *(children sit in circle)*
Made from April showers,
Tulips, buttercups,
They all pop up! *(children all jump up)*

I'M AN EASTER DUCKLING

by Susan Olson Higgins
(tune: I'm a Little Teapot)

I'm an Easter duckling,
Quack, quack, quack.
I have fluffy feathers
On my back.

You can watch my tail shake
As I go,
Waddle, waddle, waddle, waddle,
Ever so slow.

SPRING TIME IS SHOWING

by Susan Olson Higgins
(tune: Pop Goes The Weasle)

In the backyard garden plot,
> *(children crouch low to ground)*

Little flowers are growing.
> *(stand slowly)*

Up, up, they're blooming now,
> *(stand with arms held high)*

Springtime is showing!

VARIATION: Cross one arm in front of body while a flower (the other arm) grows slowly up through the soil. Keep fingers tightly together as if they were buds. Once the flowers are blooming, pop fingers open as if each were an open petal.

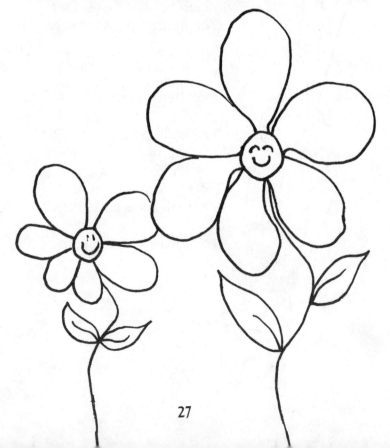

27

THE EASTER BUNNY'S HERE

by Susan Olson Higgins
(tune: Farmer In The Dell)

The Easter Bunny's here,
The Easter Bunny's here,
Heigh-ho! It's Easter Day,
The Easter Bunny's here.

The Bunny hides his eggs,
The Bunny hides his eggs,
Heigh-ho! It's Easter Day,
The Bunny hides his eggs.

Additional verses:

The children all wake up...

The children search for eggs...

They fill their baskets full...

They march in the parade...

IT'S TIME TO HIDE YOUR EGGS NOW

by Susan Olson Higgins
(tune: Are You Sleeping) (Frere Jacques)

Are you sleeping?
Are you sleeping?
(children lie sleeping on floor)

Easter Bunny,
Easter Bunny,

It's time to hide your eggs now,
Time to hide your eggs now,
(children stand up)

Hop away,
Hop away.
(children hop away)

A SPRING WALK

by Susan Olson Higgins
(tune: Baa-Baa Black Sheep)

Woolly, woolly little lamb,
Soft as can be,
Come take a Spring walk
On Easter with me.

Let's find a yellow duck,
A busy bumble bee.
Pick a four leaf clover,
Count buds on a tree.

Woolly, woolly little lamb,
Soft as can be,
Come take a Spring walk
On Easter with me.

MY EASTER BASKET

by Susan Olson Higgins
(tune: A Tisket A Tasket)

A tisket, a tasket,
I have an Easter basket. *(Hold up basket)*
Come and put an egg inside
      (Another child puts egg inside)
My pretty yellow basket.

A basket, a basket,
I have an Easter basket.
Come and put an egg inside
My pretty Easter basket.

This poem can be used in a number of ways. Here is one
possibility: Have one child walk around a circle pretending to hold
a basket while the other children pretend to place an egg in the
basket as he passes.

31

OH, EASTER BUNNY, HURRY!

by Susan Olson Higgins .
(tune: Yankee Doodle)

Little bunny bounding off,
His cotton tail flip-flopping.
He is in an Easter rush,
He has no time for stopping.

Hopping, bobbing as he goes,
Little bunny, scurry.
Hide the eggs for boys and girls,
Oh, Easter Bunny, hurry!

SUGGESTION: Some children may wish to take turns being the
Easter bunny while the others sing.

EASTERY ART

MINIATURE ART-THUMBPRINT BUNNIES

MATERIALS YOU WILL NEED

one 3½x4" piece, dark green construction paper
one 3x3½" piece light green construction paper
pink tempera paint mixed in shallow pie tin
dishpan half full of water
towel
glue

WHAT TO DO

1. Dip one thumb carefully in paint.
2. Press a bunny shape on to the 3x3" paper. (See illustration below.) Set aside to dry.
3. Rinse paint off thumb in pan of water, then dry with towel.
4. Glue the 3x3½" paper onto 3½x4" paper to make a frame around the print.

VARIATION: Make a collection of Easter eggs by thumb-printing a variety of pastel colors onto paper.

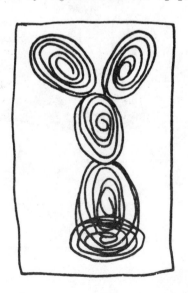

TWIST-A-WOOL BUNNY

MATERIALS YOU WILL NEED

a small amount of clean, raw wool per child
a spool of white thread
scissors
black magic marker

WHAT TO DO

1. Gently pull the wool at the top to shape it into two bunny ears.
2. Twist each bunny ear at the base one or two times, then tie it at the twist with white thread. Clip away extra thread.
3. Gently pull out a little tail on the back side of the bunny. Twist it at the base one or two times, then tie it with another white thread. Clip away extra thread.
4. Twist a tiny nose. Tie it with two or three threads at one time. Clip the threads long enough to be whiskers on either side of the bunny's nose.
5. Twist and tie any additional features you wish, such as legs, big feet or head.
6. With the black magic marker, make a dot where each of bunny's eyes should be.
7. Help the bunny hop as you read the poem, "Hoppy Bunny" on page 20 in this book.

35

PAINT EASTER CHICKS ON THE WINDOW

MATERIALS YOU WILL NEED
yellow tempera paint
green tempera paint
brush
containers for paint

WHAT TO DO
1. With yellow tempera and brush, paint a large circle on the window for the chicks' bodies. Paint another circle attached to the body for the head.
2. Add legs, wings, tail feathers, and beak.
3. Dab yellow dots on the ground for corn kernels.
4. With green tempera and brush, paint clumps of grass near the chicks.
5. After Easter, the windows should come clean using paper towels and a window washing solution.

VARIATION: Paint the Easter Bunny on the window!

POTATO PRINT EGGS

MATERIALS YOU WILL NEED:

one potato per two colors of paint
knife
several colors of thickly mixed tempera paint
one 9x9" sheet of construction paper
scissors
one paint brush for each color of tempera mixed

WHAT TO DO

1. Cut paper into a large circle which will be a plate to hold the printed eggs.
2. Using the knife, cut the potatoes in half. Be sure there is one potato half for each color of paint.
3. Dip the cut end of the potato into the paint. Press the potato onto the paper to make a print. Fill the plate with different colors of printed eggs.
4. Set aside to dry.
5. Using the paint brushes and paints, decorate the eggs with Eastery designs. Set aside to dry.

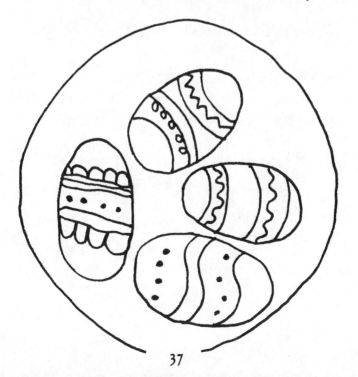

FIVE FINGER PUPPET BUNNIES

MATERIALS YOU WILL NEED:

five fingers
a fine-point felt tip pen

WHAT TO DO:

1. Read the poem, "A BUNNY FINGER PLAY," on page 15 of this book.
2. Hold up the fingers on one hand. Draw a bunny on each finger with the felt tip pen.
3. Read the poem again holding up the five, four, three, two, and one finger puppet bunnies.

BUNNY PUPPET

MATERIALS YOU WILL NEED:

one old sock
two 6x3" felt or construction paper pieces
felt tip pen
stapler or needle and thread
a rock
scissors
one cottonball

WHAT TO DO:

1. Pull the sock on your hand and draw the bunny's eyes, nose, whiskers, and mouth.
2. Cut the 6x3" felt (or paper) bunny ears.
3. Stitch the ears to the bunny, just above the bunny's eyes (or staple on the construction paper ears). Make sure no hands are inside the sock while you do this! For safety, put the rock inside the sock and sew against it.
4. Stitch or staple a cottonball on the backside for a tail.
5. Read the poem "YOU CAN BE A BUNNY" on page 10.

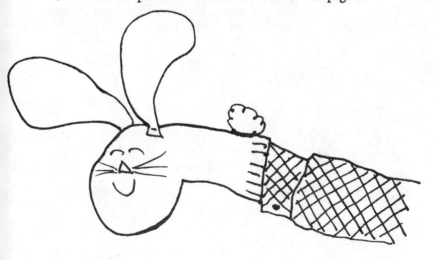

POTATO EASTER BUNNY

MATERIALS YOU WILL NEED

one potato
two raisins or marshmallows
nine toothpicks
two precut 6x2" construction paper bunny ears
one cottonball

WHAT TO DO

1. Stand the potato upright. Push two toothpicks into the potato for bunny legs. Adjust them so the bunny will sit (not stand) by himself.
2. Break one toothpick in half and push each half into the potato for bunny arms.
3. Break two toothpicks in half and push them into the potato near the nose for bunny whiskers.
4. Break another toothpick in half and push the two halves into the potato to hold the eyes. Push a raisin on each toothpick for eyes.
5. Push each bunny ear onto a toothpick. Push each toothpick into the potato so the bunny ears will stand tall.
6. Secure the bunny's cottonball tail to the potato with another toothpick. The tail may also be used to support the bunny so he sits upright.

BUNNY EARS, BUNNY NOSE AND BUNNY TAIL

MATERIALS YOU WILL NEED:

two 2x12" strips white construction paper
stapler
four 4x12" strips white construction paper
old newspaper
black tempera paint
paint brush
scissors
masking tape and cotton

WHAT TO DO

1. Staple the two 2x12" strips together to begin making a headband. Measure the head size with the strip, then staple the ends together.
2. Put the four 4x12" strips together and cut them into bunny ears. Two strips together will make one bunny ear.
3. Wrinkle a small amount of old newspaper to stuff between the front and back strip of each bunny ear. Staple the stuffing into each ear around the edges.
4. Staple the ears onto the head band.
5. Paint a triangle, black bunny nose on the child's nose with tempera paint. (Make sure the child's skin is not sensitive to the paint.)
6. Pull a handful of cotton into a bunny tail shape. Attach it with masking tape to the "bunny's" backside.
7. Read the poem, "YOU CAN BE A BUNNY," on page 10 while the children act it out in their bunny ears, bunny nose and bunny tails.

Bunny Ears

SPRING WORM ON A BROAD LEAF

MATERIALS YOU WILL NEED

six multi-colored 2x6" strips construction paper
paste
felt tip pens
one 12x18" green sheet construction paper
scissors

WHAT TO DO

1. Roll each of the six paper strips into a circle and paste the ends together.
2. Set to six circles one in front of the other to make the worm. Paste them together.
3. Draw a face on the first circle.
4. Cut a large leaf from the green paper.
5. Glue to worm onto the leaf.

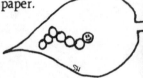

EASTER BUBBLES

MATERIALS YOU WILL NEED

one part liquid detergent
one part glycerine (found in most drug stores)
five parts distilled water
one wire coat hanger or any wire for a frame
cake pan

WHAT TO DO

1. Mix the bubble-making ingredients in the cake pan.
2. Bend the coat hanger, or wire, into the shape of a circle with a handle.
3. Dip the wire into the bubble mixture, then gently move it through the air to make beautiful, Eastery bubbles!

BOOKMARKER GIFT IN AN EASTER CARD

MATERIALS YOU WILL NEED

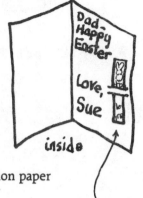

    multi-colors of tissue paper
    green yarn
    felt tip pen
    9x12" sheet construction paper
    5x5" piece scrap paper
    white glue
    scissors
    pencil or pen
    one 2x6" piece of construction paper
    one yellow or pink 2" square construction paper
    one green 1x5" strip construction paper

WHAT TO DO:

1. Cut the multi-colored tissue paper into 2x2" squares
2. Fold the 9x12" construction paper in half to make the card.
3. Draw a flower or duck or cross on the front of the card. Make it a simple design.
4. Squeeze a small amount of white glue onto a piece of scrap paper.
5. Wrinkle the tissue paper into tiny balls, then one square at a time, dip them in the glue, and place them within the lines of the design until it is filled with tissue balls.
6. Cut a green stem or duck legs from the yarn, if needed. Attach with glue. The front of the card is finished.
7. Open the card. Make two 2" horizontal slits with the scissors on the backside of the card where the bookmarker will slide in. Make the slits close to one side of the card - this leaves room to write a message.
8. With the 2" square of construction paper, cut out an Easter flower, or duck, or chick, or bunny.
9. Glue it to the top of the bookmarker.
10. If you cut a flower, add a green stem cut from the 1x5" strip of green construction paper.
11. Write an Easter message inside the card with the felt tip pens. Sign the card with the pen or pencil.
12. Give the card to someone you love for Easter!

CHICKEN IN A NEST

MATERIALS YOU WILL NEED:

> brown paper bag, small lunch size
> old newspaper
> red, yellow, orange, and brown construction paper
> scissors
> stapler
> glue
> string

WHAT TO DO

1. Stuff the paper bag full of old newspaper strips.
2. Twist the open end of the bag, then tie it to make the neck and head of the chicken.
3. Cut tail feathers, beak, wings, wattle, and eggs from the construction paper you have on hand.
4. Attach the above parts to the chicken with glue.
5. Cut strips of yellow construction paper to make "straw" for the nest. Glue the stips together to look like a nest.
6. Set the "eggs" you have cut in the nest, then set the chicken on top of the eggs.

44

EASTER SUNRISE IN PASTEL CHALK

MATERIALS YOU WILL NEED:

one 12x18" sheet yellow construction paper
pastel chalks

WHAT TO DO:
1. Discuss the colors seen in the sky at sunrise, and how the sun colors everything...flowers, trees, buildings, lakes...soft colors at that time of day. Allow the children to describe sunrises they have seen.
2. Give the children chalk and paper to create their own sunrise scene, as they think it will look on Easter morning.

BUNNY ME!

MATERIALS YOU WILL NEED:

roll of white butcher paper
pencil
scissors

WHAT TO DO:
1. Roll out the paper and cut it the length of the child, plus bunny ears.
2. Have the child lie down on his paper while another child traces around his body with the pencil. Be sure to add tall bunny ears where they belong!
3. Each child cuts out his own bunny. Add any creative details or features you wish, with any media you have available.
4. Read the poem, "A BUNNY WHO IS FUNNY," on page 12 of this book when the project is completed. Display the bunnies.

CHICK IN AN EGG SHELL

MATERIALS YOU WILL NEED
   ball of yellow yarn
   one 1½" cardboard square
   one 2" cardboard square
   scissors
   two clean, dry, broken egg shell halves
   white glue
   two tiny ½" orange felt triangles

WHAT TO DO
1. Wrap yellow yarn around the 1½" cardboard square 20 times. Take the yarn off the cardboard. With one 8" length of yellow yarn, tie a knot tightly in the center of the yarn wrap. Do NOT trim the long strings hanging from the 8" yarn.
2. Cut the loops of each of the yarn wraps in the center. Fluff the yarn around to make a small yarn ball.
3. Wrap yellow yarn around the 2" cardboard square 25 times. Take the yarn off the cardboard. With the other 8" length of yellow yarn, tie a knot tightly in the center of the yarn wrap. Again, do NOT trim the long strings hanging from the 8" yarn.
4. Cut the loops of each of the yarn wraps in the center. Fluff the yarn around to make larger yarn ball.
5. Tie the long strings of the smaller and the larger yarn balls together to make the head and body of the chick. Be sure to tie them securely. Now trim off long strands of yarn.
6. Glue the two felt triangles on the head for a beak.
7. Glue one egg shell on top of the chick's head.
8. Glue a short piece of yarn in a circle on the bottom of the shell to keep the shell from rolling over when you set it down.

BUTTERFLY NET

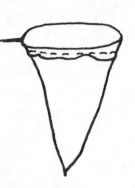

MATERIALS YOU WILL NEED

one wire coat hanger
one 30x30x30" triangle of cheesecloth
masking tape
needle
thread
scissors
an adult to supervise hanger bending

WHAT TO DO

1.   Open the coat hanger so it is straight.
2.   Reshape it so it has a circular frame and a handle. Cover the handle with masking tape so sharp edges will not cut.
3.   Stitch the cheesecloth over the circular part of the wire.
4.   Stitch down the side of the net to close it.
5.   Go outside and try your net. See if you can catch a Spring butterfly... then let it go, of course!

FOOTPRINT BUNNY EARS

MATERIALS YOU WILL NEED:

12x18" sheet blue construction paper
white tempera paint mixed in a large shallow pan
brush
paper towels
basin of water
chair

WHAT TO DO:

1.   Paint an Easter bunny with white paint and brush.
2.   Remove socks and shoes. Step into the pan of paint, one foot at a time. Press each foot onto the paper to make bunny footprint ears.
3.   Step into the basin of water to clean the feet. Dry them with a paper towel. Place a chair near the basin of water to sit on while cleaning feet.

EASTER BONNET

MATERIALS YOU WILL NEED

one white paper plate 9'' diameter with fluted edges
one 9'' circle of colorful fabric
white glue
water
paint brush
scissors
stapler
two 12'' ribbons or yarn lengths

WHAT TO DO:

1. Mix a small amount of white glue with a few drops of water to thin the consistency of the glue.
2. With the paint brush, paint one side of the paper plate with the glue.
3. Lay the circle of fabric on the plate. Set aside to dry.
4. With the scissors, cut a straight line to the center of the plate.
5. Overlap the edges where the cut has been made and staple them together.
6. Turn up the fluted edges for an upturned brim on the hat.
7. Cut 1'' slits on opposite sides of the hat for the ties to fit through.
8. Push the ribbons or yarn lengths through the slits. Either staple them or tie knots in the ends above the brim to hold them in place.
9. Read the poem, ''WHAT IS IT?'' on page 17 of this book.

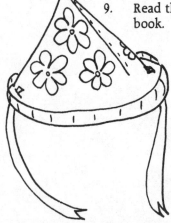

GIGANTIC BOUQUET OF FLOWERS

MATERIALS YOU WILL NEED:

3x3' butcher paper
12x18" white construction paper
blue tempera paint and brush
colored chalk
scissors
glue

WHAT TO DO:

1. Cut the butcher paper into the shape of a vase or flower bowl.
2. Paint the vase blue.
3. Draw one or more flowers with chalk on the 12x18" construction paper.
4. Cut out each flower.
5. Glue the flowers to the vase so that they appear to be inside it.

TISSUE PAPER EGGS

MATERIALS YOU WILL NEED

one hard-boiled egg
1" squares of tissue paper, any color
white glue
paint brush
egg carton

WHAT TO DO

1. Paint glue on the hard-boiled egg.
2. Lay tissue squares on the glue-covered egg until the egg is covered with tissue.
3. Set the egg into the egg carton to dry.

WEAVE AN EGG

MATERIALS YOU WILL NEED

one 12x18" sheet construction paper
scissors
glue
ribbons, yarn, colorful string, or ½" widths of material
scraps cut in 12" lengths
newspaper
razor blade
an adult to supervise use of razor

WHAT TO DO

1. Cut the 12x18" construction paper into the shape of a large egg.
2. Lay the egg on a thickness of newspaper. With the razor blade, cut 1" vertical slits in rows across the egg leaving a 1" border of paper at the edge. Cut an even number of vertical slits in each row.
3. Weave the 12" ribbons or strips over and under and through the slits cut in the egg.
4. Trim the ends of the ribbon so they are even with the edge of the egg. Glue the ends down.

EGG BABY

MATERIALS YOU WILL NEED:

one hard-boiled egg
felt tip pen
white glue
one 4x4" colorful fabric square

WHAT TO DO:

1. Draw a tiny face near the top of the egg with the felt tip pen.
2. Fold the fabric square around the egg like a baby blanket, gluing each corner as you set it in place.

50

MRS. HOWELL'S
CELLOPHANE BUMBLEBEE

MATERIALS YOU WILL NEED

two 9x12" sheets yellow construction paper
scissors
glue
four pieces colored cellophane approximately 4x5"
black construction paper scraps
string

WHAT TO DO

1. Put the two sheets of construction paper together and cut out two bumblebees at the same time.
2. Cut away holes for eyes and one spot on each wing.
3. Insert the cellophane between the front and back of the bumblebee (in the center) and glue it to both sides. Hold everything together until dry.
4. Add extra details such as black stripes, eye balls, antennae, legs, or stinger, using the black construction paper scraps.
5. With the string, hang the bumblebees in the window so the light will filter through the cellophane wings and eyes.

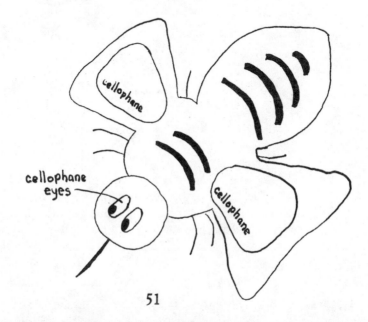

APPLE BLOSSOM BRANCH

MATERIALS YOU WILL NEED

small branch or twig that will lie flat on paper
white glue
12x18" green construction paper
3x3" squares of pink tissue paper

WHAT TO DO

1. Glue the branch or twig flat on the 12x18" construction paper.
2. Fold and twist the center of the tissue squares to make a "stem" for the blossoms. Glue the center of the twisted "stem" to the branch or to the paper next to the branch. Set aside to dry flat.

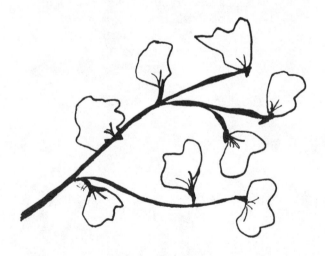

VARIATION: Paint the stem on the construction paper with brown tempera paint, then glue the blossoms onto the painted branches.

CHARCOAL A BUNNY

MATERIALS YOU WILL NEED

charcoal
9x12" construction paper
cotton
glue

WHAT TO DO

1. Charcoal a bunny on the paper. You may wish to use oval shapes to create the bunny's body parts.
2. Glue a cotton tail onto the bunny.

MURAL OF AN EASTER EGG PARADE

MATERIALS YOU WILL NEED

variety of tempera paint colors
brushes for each color
approximately 6 feet of butcher paper
newspaper

WHAT TO DO

1. Lay newspaper down to protect the work area. Prepare the tempera paints. Roll out the butcher paper on top of the newspaper.
2. Have each child paint a picture of an Easter egg marching in the parade.
3. To avoid drips, set aside to dry before hanging the mural.

SAND DUCK

MATERIALS YOU WILL NEED

small container of fine sand
white glue slightly diluted with water
12x18" construction paper
paint brush
yellow and orange tempera paint
newspaper
pencil

WHAT TO DO

1. Cover the working area with newspaper
2. Place the 12x18" construction paper on the newspaper.
3. With the pencil, draw a large duck.
4. Paint the duck with the diluted white glue.
5. Sprinkle sand on the duck. Set aside to dry.
6. Paint the duck yellow. Paint the duck's bill and webbed feet orange.
7. If you wish to add other details, paint green grass and flowers to the bottom of the page near the duck's feet.

BUNNY GAMES

SPRINGTIME LEAPFROG

MATERIALS YOU WILL NEED

two or more children

HOW TO PLAY

1. Choose one child to be the leaper.
2. Have the other children crouch down low to the ground, curling up in a tight ball with their heads tucked to their knees. They should form a straight line with about one foot between them.
3. Have the leaper place his hands on the center of the back of the last child in line as he leaps over the top.
4. Leaper continues down the row until he is at the head of the line. Then he crouches low to join the line.
5. The last child in the line now has a turn to be the leaper. He leaps over the backs of the children in the row until he is at the head of the line.
6. Continue until all of the children have had a turn being the LEAPFROG.

BUNNY OBSTACLE COURSE

MATERIALS YOU WILL NEED

string
lots of obstacles
hard-boiled eggs — one per player

HOW TO PLAY

1. Lay the string down to mark a course over, under, around, through, and beside obstacles such as trees, equipment, boxes, ropes, etc.
2. Choose a leader to take the children on the obstacle course, following the path of the string.
3. The children must carry an egg.

BUNNY FIND YOUR BURROW

MATERIALS YOU WILL NEED:

two precut construction paper eggs per child with the same Easter word written on each egg, such as:

egg   egg   bunny   bunny   hop   hop

HOW TO PLAY:

1. While the children are not looking, hide one of each construction paper egg in a designated area.
2. Call the children together. Give each child an egg.
3. Explain they will have to find their "burrows" by finding another egg with the same word on it. The only way they can travel is by hopping. When the bunnies find their matching eggs, they have found their "burrows." They must stay in their "burrows" until ALL of the bunnies have found their matching eggs. The first bunny to find his burrow is the winner and can help hide the eggs for the next game.
4. When all of the bunnies have found their "burrows," the leader should call, "Bunnies, come to the garden for carrots," and all of the bunnies must hop back to the starting place for the next game.

BUNNY TAIL TAG

MATERIALS YOU WILL NEED

one cottonball per child
masking tape

HOW TO PLAY

1. Tape one cottonball on the backside of each child playing the game, except the child who is "IT."
2. The child who is "IT" chases the other players until he can snatch the bunny tail from one of the players.
3. The player who lost his bunny tail must help "IT" snatch other bunny tails. Anyone who looses a tail must help "IT" snatch other tails.
4. The last player to loose his or her tail is "IT" for the next game of BUNNY TAIL TAG.

VARIATION: Make a rule that all players must jump rather than run.

FY LITTLE BUNNY —
A Wiggle-With-Me Story

haring this story with the children, read the
ig dialogue aloud, so they learn the actions which
ond with the words. Be sure to demonstrate the
ls, then give the children a chance to practice them
before the story begins. If necessary, break down individual
movements per group.

Whenever I say the word "**cottontail**,"
  shake your bottom.
Whenever I say "**pink nose**,"
  wrinkle your nose like a bunny.
Whenever I say "**soft, brown eyes**,"
  blink your eyes three times.
Whenever I say "**long, tall ears**,"
  hold your arms over your head and wiggle your hands.
Whenever I say "**hopped**,"
  and that will be only one time, hop away to wherever
  you wish. Go quietly, and be careful not to bump other
  bunnies as you hop!

Now, here's the story. Listen carefully and do not forget
your part!

Once upon a time there was a fluffy little bunny who
lived in a safe burrow deep under the roots of a great old
tree on the edge of the forest. The fluffy little bunny had a
pink nose, a **cottontail**, **soft, brown eyes**, and **long, tall
ears** that could hear any sound for miles around.

One day when the bunny was bounding through the
forest with his little **cottontail** bobbing along behind him,
he came upon a bubbling brook. He stopped and perked up
his **long, tall ears** to listen for any sounds that might tell
him of danger. He sniffed the air with his **pink nose** for the
scent of an enemy. His **soft, brown eyes** looked in every
direction.

58

His long, tall ears told him nothing. His pink nose told him nothing. His soft, brown eyes saw no sign of another creature anywhere. So the bunny bounced off through the forest with his cottontail bobbing behind him.

The bunny had not gone far when he came upon a fallen log blocking his path. Again he stopped and perked up his long, tall ears to listen for any sound that might tell him of danger. He sniffed the air with his pink nose for the scent of an enemy. His soft, brown eyes looked in every direction.

His long, tall ears told him nothing. His pink nose told him nothing. His soft, brown eyes saw no sign of another creature anywhere. So, the bunny bounced off through the forest with his cottontail bobbing behind him.

Suddenly, there was a snap of a twig. The cottontail stopped bobbing. The bunny's long, tall ears perked up to listen for the sound of a stranger. He sniffed the air with his pink nose for any scent of danger. His soft, brown eyes looked in every direction.

Then, there it was! It moved quietly through the forest on the same path where the bunny stood. It was coming closer and closer. The bunny did not move. It began feeling frightened!

Who should come bounding down the path . . . but another little bunny just like him! She had a pink nose, a cottontail, soft, brown eyes, and long, tall ears that could hear for miles around. She stopped and looked at the bunny with her soft, brown eyes. They smiled at each other. Then they turned, and they hopped off down the path together.

SKIP ON SPRING BLOSSOMS

MATERIALS YOU WILL NEED
music record
record player
one construction paper flower per child
masking tape
an adult to supervise the record player

HOW TO PLAY
1. Tape flowers on the floor in a circle, one for each player.
2. Turn on the music. While the music plays, the children skip around all of the flowers in one direction.
3. With no warning, lift the arm of the record player to stop the music. At that instant, the children must scurry to find a flower to stand on.
4. When you begin the music again, the children will skip until the next time it stops.
5. Once the children are familiar with this procedure, go on to the next part of the game. Every time you stop the music, take one of the flowers away from the circle. That will leave one extra child without a flower to stand on each time the music stops, like musical chairs. The extra child should go to the outside of the circle and sit with the others caught without a flower. Continue until there is only one child left in the center... the winner!
6. Children LOVE this game!!

JELLY BEAN GUESS

MATERIALS YOU WILL NEED

one or two bags of jelly beans
one large glass jar and lid
paper and pencil

HOW TO PLAY

1. Count the jelly beans as you put them in the jar (while no one is looking).
2. Then, show the jelly bean jar to the children. Explain they will have to guess how many jelly beans are in the jar. The one closest to the exact amount is the winner. Record the guesses on the paper.
3. On the day you have designated, announce the winner!
4. Pass out the jelly beans for a chewy treat, or save for the JELLY BEAN RELAY described below.

JELLY BEAN RELAY

MATERIALS YOU WILL NEED

the children divided into relay teams
three jelly beans per team
one spoon per child (ruler for older children)
two boundaries marked 12 feet across from each other

HOW TO PLAY

1. Divide each team in half with an equal number of players behind each goal line. Players line up single file and face center.
2. Each player should have his or her own spoon.
3. Give the first player three jelly beans to carry on the spoon to the player on his team on the opposite side. That player returns with the jelly beans in his spoon. Continue until all of the players have had a turn and are sitting on the side opposite from where they started.
4. The first team to have all team members carry the jelly beans to the opposite side is the winner!

DON'T BREAK THE EGGS!

MATERIALS YOU WILL NEED

one balloon per child
precut 2" construction paper eggs—3 per child

HOW TO PLAY

1. Blow up one balloon per child and pass balloons out.
2. Explain that these are not really balloons, but rather "eggs." If these "eggs" touch the floor, they will break. Each time an "egg" breaks, the player will receive a construction paper egg.
3. Set a timer for one minute or count slowly to 20 while the children try to keep their balloons in the air. If a balloon touches the ground, give that child a construction paper egg.
4. At the end of the time, the child with the fewest construction paper eggs is the winner!

VARIATION: Tie a string across the room. Divide players into two teams. Bat the balloon over the string to play a "balloon" volleyball game.

*OR...play an indoor baseball game using empty two-liter soda bottles at bats and balloons as balls.

FILL YOUR EASTER BASKET

MATERIALS YOU WILL NEED

> precut construction paper eggs, five of one color per child
> an Easter basket

HOW TO PLAY

1. Give each player five eggs of the same color. If possible, each player should have a different color.
2. Assign each player an area where he or she will search for another player's hidden eggs.
3. Also assign each player a small area in which to hide the five eggs. Allow time to hide them.
4. When all the eggs are hidden, call, "Fill your Easter basket!" The children then switch areas and move to the place where they are to search for another player's eggs.
5. There is no winner... just lots of giggling and calling "I found one!"

Area II
(hide 5 red eggs here)

a I
(hide 5 blue eggs here)

Area III
(hide 5 yellow eggs here)

GIVE BUNNY A TAIL

MATERIALS YOU WILL NEED:

> 5-ft. bunny cut from butcher paper
> large cottonballs
> masking tape
> scarf

HOW TO PLAY:

1. Tape the large bunny to the wall or door.
2. Have all of the children stand aside in a group and come up to play one at a time.
3. Cover the player's eyes with the scarf.
4. Hand the player a cottonball with masking tape on the back of it.
5. Point the player in the right direction towards the bunny, where he or she will tape the tail on.
6. The player coming closest to the bunny's tail is the winner.

QUACK, QUACK, WADDLE RACE

MATERIALS YOU WILL NEED:

two lines 10 feet apart (the start and finish lines)

HOW TO PLAY:

1. All players line up behind the starting line, squatting low to the ground like a duck.
2. At the signal "go," all of the "ducks" duck-walk or waddle to the opposite line, quacking as loudly as they can.
3. The first duck to waddle across the finish line is the winner.

VARIATION: Waddle down to the finish line and run back to the starting line for a longer race.

JELLY BEAN SHAKE

MATERIALS YOU WILL NEED

one glass Coke or soda bottle filled with
different colored jelly beans

HOW TO PLAY

1. Players should sit in a circle.
2. Pass the bottle around the circle, stopping at each player, giving him a chance to shake one (and only one) jelly bean out of the bottle.
3. The first player to have four jelly beans the same color is the winner!

BUNNY RECIPES

Bunny's
Carrot
Patch

BUNNY'S FAVORITE...
SLICED CARROTS
INGREDIENTS YOU WILL NEED

one or more raw carrots
potato peeler
sharp knife
an adult to supervise cutting and peeling

WHAT TO DO
1. Wash your carrot(s) thoroughly.
2. With the potato peeler, peel away the outside layer of the carrot. Always peel in the direction away from your hand.
3. With the knife, cut off both carrot ends.
4. You had better make two... just in case the bunny hears you munching and crunching and wants one, too.

EGG IN A BASKET

INGREDIENTS YOU WILL NEED
one egg
one slice of bread
butter
one average sized water glass
knife
skillet
spatula
an adult to supervise cooking

WHAT TO DO
1. Press the lip of the glass to the center of the slice of bread. Push down hard to cut out the center of the bread and leave a circular hole where the egg will sit.
2. Butter both sides of the bread as well as the center piece cut out from the bread.
3. Place the skillet on the burner, medium low heat.
4. Butter the bottom of the skillet.
5. Place the bread and the bread circle in the skillet. Let each side brown for a minute or two, flipping them with the spatula.
6. Crack and open the egg into the center hole of the slice of bread. Fry the egg with the bread until it is done to taste.
7. While the egg is frying, cook and flip the center circle of the bread to make toast.
8. When the egg is fried on both sides, take it up and serve the egg in its basket!

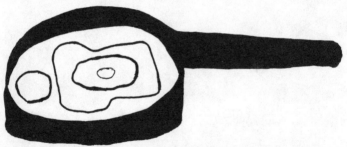

BUNNIED EGGS

INGREDIENTS YOU WILL NEED

six hard-boiled eggs
a pinch of salt
a pinch of pepper
a shake of paprika
salad dressing
bowl
knife
fork
box of raisins

WHAT TO DO

1. Slice the hard-boiled eggs in half lengthwise.
2. Remove the yolks and place them in a bowl.
3. Mash the yolks with a fork.
4. Add a shake of salt and pepper to the yolks.
5. Add enough salad dressing for the yolk mixture to hold together. Mash it in with a fork.
6. Stuff each egg half with the yolk mixture.
7. Sprinkle one shake of paprika on the egg yolk.
8. Arrange three raisins on top of the yolk in the shape of a bunny.
9. This is a perfect after-the-bunny's-visit treat!

BUNNY CHEESE SANDWICH

INGREDIENTS YOU WILL NEED

    bread slices
    cheese
    butter
    stuffed green olives
    bunny shaped cookie cutter
    flat cookie pan
    oven
    knife
    an adult to supervise cutting

WHAT TO DO

1. Cut the bread into bunny shapes with the cookie cutter. Butter the bunny bread.
2. Slice the cheese and lay it on the bunny bread.
3. Slice one olive in half and place it on the cheese where the tail of the bunny should be.
4. Place the bunny bread sandwich on the cookie pan, then into the moderately heated oven. Allow the cheese to melt. Serve while warm.

FROSTED EASTER GRAPES

INGREDIENTS YOU WILL NEED

    two egg whites
    seedless green grapes
    powered sugar
    waxed paper
    wire rack

WHAT TO DO

1. Wash the grapes and set them aside to dry.
2. Beat the egg whites until they are foamy and light.
3. Separate the grapes into tiny bunches.
4. Lay out waxed paper under your working area.
5. Dip the grapes into the egg white. Shake off excess drips.
6. Dip grapes into a mound of powdered sugar on the waxed paper. Make sure each grape is covered with the sugar. Shake off excess sugar, then dip again, and again until the grapes are completely covered.
7. Set the grapes aside to dry on the wire rack. When they are dry, they will look like beautiful, crystal Easter eggs.

DAFFODIL CAKE

INGREDIENTS YOU WILL NEED

6 eggs
3/4 cup sugar
1/2 cup sugar
3 T. water
1 cup flour
1 heaping t. baking powder
2 mixing bowls
electric mixer
spoon
angle food cake pan greased and floured
oven
an adult to supervise measuring

WHAT TO DO

1. Separate egg whites from the egg yolks.
2. Beat the egg whites until light and fluffy.
3. Add and beat in 3/4 cup sugar to egg whites.
4. In separate bowl, beat egg yolks (while adding 1/2 cup sugar and 3 T. water) until stiff.
5. Sift flour and baking powder and mix half in the white mixture and half in the yellow mixture.
6. Put the white mixture in the bottom of the angel food cake pan and the yellow mixture on top.
7. Bake the 45 minutes at 325°.

NATURALLY DYED EASTER EGGS

INGREDIENTS YOU WILL NEED
two cups water
eggs
onion skins, tea, or blueberries
pan
stove top
an adult to supervise stove use

WHAT TO DO
1. Place the eggs in a pan with the water on the stove top.
2. Add either onion skins, tea, or blueberries to the water with the eggs. Note: Onion skins will color eggs yellow, tea will color eggs brown, and blueberries will color the eggs blue.
3. Bring the water to boil, then slow boil for at least 7 minutes.
4. Allow the eggs to sit in the water until they pick up the coloring of the water. Blueberries will take the longest for the color to set.

VARIATION: Try boiling the petals of various flowers with the eggs to see if they will color. Pansies color eggs soft yellow, for example.

Credits

The Kindergarten Co-op

Carol Hooper

Mrs. Barbara Lapp

The Redding Co-op Preschool

Bill Olson

Louise Taylor

Charlie and Gillian Trumbull

Grant Elementary School

Kenneth Adams

Reverend Benjamin Pent

To each of you,
thank you for your input and ideas!

For information on how to order additional books, write to:

PUMPKIN PRESS PUBLISHING HOUSE
P.O. BOX 139
SHASTA, CA 96087

THE TAIL END . . . . . .

See You Next Year!!!